31 DAYS OF GRATITUDE

WRITTEN BY

Mart Tweedy

CANNYCRYSTALS.CO.UK
CANNYCRYSTALSACADEMY.CO.UK
@CANNYCRYSTALS

Dedicated to
Ken Dobson

INTRODUCTION

Welcome to the 31 Days of Gratitude!

When we practice gratitude daily, it can really help to change the way we look at, and perceive things in our lives. But not only that, it can also help us to raise our vibrations to assist with manifesting everything we desire in life.

Manifesting and gratitude are both related to the Law of Attraction, which is the idea that your thoughts and emotions can attract positive or negative experiences into your life.

Gratitude is a powerful tool for manifesting because it helps you to focus on the positive aspects of your life and attract more of what you appreciate. When you're grateful for what you have, you send out positive vibrations that attract more of the same. By focusing on what you're thankful for, you can shift your mindset from one of lack to one of abundance and attract even more abundance into your life.

In addition, manifesting often involves visualising the things you want to manifest and feeling as though you have already received them. Gratitude can help you to feel the positive emotions associated with having the things you desire, which can make it easier to manifest them in your life. When you feel grateful for something as if you already have it, you raise your vibration and attract more of that energy into your life.

Overall, gratitude is a powerful tool for manifesting because it helps you to focus on the positive aspects of your life and attract more of what you appreciate.

Not only assisting with your manifestation dreams, practising gratitude also has numerous benefits for our physical, emotional, and mental well-being.

It can seriously improve your mental health - gratitude has been linked to decreased symptoms of depression and anxiety, and improved overall mental health. It helps to foster positive emotions and reduce negative emotions, leading to an increased sense of well-being.

It's also been known to boost your physical health - grateful people have been found to have lower blood pressure, better sleep quality, and stronger immune systems. They are also more likely to engage in healthy behaviours such as exercise and self-care.

You can experience enhanced relationships – expressing gratitude towards others can strengthen relationships by increasing feelings of connection, empathy, and social support. It can also promote forgiveness and reduce feelings of resentment.

It increases resilience - gratitude can help us cope with stress and adversity by fostering a more positive outlook and increasing our ability to find meaning and purpose in difficult situations.

And last, but by no means least, it improves self-esteem - grateful people tend to have higher levels of self-esteem and self-worth. By focusing on what we have rather than what we lack, we can cultivate a more positive self-image.

Overall, practising gratitude can have a profound impact on our lives and help us lead happier, healthier, and more fulfilling lives.

When done on a daily basis, gratitude can be a great way to improve your overall well-being and happiness.

Here are some practical ways to incorporate gratitude into your daily routine:

Keep a gratitude journal: Take a few minutes each day to write down three things you are grateful for. They can be simple things like having a roof over your head, a warm meal, or spending time with loved ones. Writing them down can help you focus on the positive things in your life.

Express gratitude to others: Take time to thank the people around you who have made a positive impact on your life. This can be as simple as sending a text or writing a note of thanks to a friend or family member.

Practice mindfulness: During meditation or prayer, take a few minutes to focus on the things you are grateful for in your life. This can help you feel more centred and content.

Focus on the present moment: Be mindful of the present moment and try not to get too caught up in worrying about the future or dwelling on the past. Focusing on the present can help you appreciate the things you have right now.

Use positive affirmations: Start your day by saying a positive affirmation to yourself, such as "I am grateful for all the good things in my life" or "I am thankful for the people who support me."

By incorporating these simple practices into your daily routine, you can cultivate a sense of gratitude that will help you stay positive and happy even during difficult times, and these are exactly some of the things we're going to be exploring over the next 31 days.

As my way of thanking you for buying this book, you can also grab one of the Canny Crystals Well-being Journals to work through alongside this challenge, at 20% off by using discount code **GRATITUDE** at cannycrystals.co.uk

So without further ado, grab a pen, get yourself comfortable and let's begin...

DAY 1

What Makes You Happy?

Hello, and welcome to day 1 of the 31 Days of Gratitude challenge. If you've joined in with these 31 days, then you're already committed to making a real difference in your life. So go ahead and give yourself a pat on the back for that at the very least. A massive well done from me too!

As we all know, making a change in your life can be quite daunting to some people, so by breaking this down into 31 smaller chunks, it's more sustainable for you to keep up and continue doing the gratitude work long after you've come to day 31 and finished.

So let's set some intentions for the 31 days ahead because it's my intention that over the next 31 days, we're going to look at your current gratitude practice and elevate it to new heights.

For those of you that have read a book called The Magic, every single day you're asked to write down 10 things to be grateful for, which leads to 280 things across the 28-day process. And rightly so, if I asked you right now to list 280 things to be grateful for, many of you I dare say, would get stuck at around 10-20 gratitude statements.

So it's also my intention that by the end of this 31-day challenge, you're going to really have your eyes opened to all the different things that you can be grateful for, as well as look at how gratitude can impact and benefit your life.

We all know that the more we do something, the more likely it is to become a part of who we are, and it's then more likely to become part of our daily routine. This will ultimately help to shape who we are as we'll be benefiting from the energy that gratitude gives us.

Let's look at gratitude before we make a start. What do I mean by gratitude, and being grateful? I define it as a simple technique to put an intentional focus on the things that we appreciate around us in everyday life, it's seeing the abundance in every situation instead of allowing it to become normalised and put to the back of our minds.

We know that when we experience something day in, day out, it really does become the norm for us. The whole point of this 31-day challenge, therefore, is to incorporate gratitude into our everyday activities, to the point where it actually becomes standard practice.

It allows us to tap into the abundance that surrounds us already, instead of living in the lack or scarcity mindset of never having enough. It can help to shift your mindset from being a pessimist and having their glass half empty, to someone who sees their glass as half full and is full of optimism.

When we allow that abundance and positivity to become the norm for us, we allow those impactful energies into our lives, which helps us to be, do, and have all the things that we want in life.

Gratitude can really change ordinary opportunities into life-changing experiences, it all depends on how you look at them, and what eyes you look at them through.

So I want you to grab yourself a pen, and you're going to use this book (or a journal if you prefer) for the whole 31 days, just don't be grabbing any scrap bits of paper! Each day we're going to ask ourselves a different question, alongside three set questions.

The three questions we're going to journal and answer daily across the 31 days are:
- What is something that made me smile yesterday?
- What can I do to make myself feel good and love myself today? And...
- What is one thing that I'm grateful for today?

So once you've got sorted, you've written those three questions down in your journal, just take a few moments to get comfortable with wherever you are, whether you're in bed, at your office, at a table, in the gym... wherever you are, get comfy, check in with yourself.

Take a few deep breaths and ask yourself those questions internally. Feel free to use your journal and pen to write down your answers, or if you prefer, you can write them down on the following pages, or just answer them internally in your head.

If you're tech-savvy, you could even write them down in the notes app on your phone, or on a tablet, or laptop... whatever feels best for you!

Most people like to write exercises like this down as when they're feeling a little deflated, or simply having an "off-day" they can look back at what they wrote, and their answers will also serve as a little pick me up.

So our question for today's practice, for day 1 is this... "what makes me happy?"

Now you might be thinking, that's a really simple question to answer, but it should really get your thought cogs turning and delve deep into what's working for you, what's going your way, and what makes you feel good inside.

I'd like you to spend a good 5-10 minutes writing down or speaking out what makes you happy, from little things such as seeing a puppy wagging its tail, to larger things such as having hot water to enable you to take a shower. Write down as much as you can possibly think of.

When you give focus to those feelings of happiness and gratitude, that's what's going to really transform your life and transform the way that you're feeling. Remember, when we feel good on the inside, we radiate those good feelings of positivity on the outside too.

So I'm going to leave you there on that thought for today, but I'm really, really excited to hear what you journal for your three main questions, as well as your daily thought-provoking question.

Feel free to take a picture of your daily answers if you're feeling brave enough to share, use the hashtag #31daysofgratitude and tag my main account on social media which is @cannycrystals, and I look forward to seeing you all again tomorrow for day 2.

WHAT IS SOMETHING THAT MADE ME SMILE YESTERDAY?

....

....

....

WHAT CAN I DO TO MAKE MYSELF FEEL GOOD AND LOVE MYSELF TODAY?

....

....

....

WHAT IS ONE THING THAT I'M GRATEFUL FOR TODAY?

....

....

....

WHAT MAKES ME HAPPY?

....

....

....

DAY 2

Learning From Challenges

Welcome back to day 2. Just before we start, let's allow ourselves to really be present in this moment. If you can, sit comfortably with both feet on the floor and your back straight. If it feels good to do so, you can close your eyes, and then I just want you to take a big deep breath in.

As you breathe out, just notice how it feels to be inside your body right now. Notice how it feels to be sat there, feeling into the peaceful nature of this present moment, which will allow the gratitude to build up inside of you and then read the following quote:

"Develop an attitude of gratitude, giving thanks for everything that happens to you, knowing that every step forward is a step toward achieving something bigger and better than your current situation."

Really feel what bubbles up inside of you from reading that, and once you've sat on that feeling, whenever you're ready to, you can take one last deep breath and move on with todays task.

You know by now that each day we're going to answer our 3 main questions, which are also on the following pages:
- What is something that made me smile yesterday?
- What can I do to make myself feel good and love myself today? And...
- What is 1 thing that I'm grateful for today?

But today's thought-provoking question to add to this is: how can I learn from the daily challenges in my life?

A lot of people will just assume that they're tested and challenged every single day, and to some extent, this is true. We're all tested in some way, shape or form daily. But what can we learn from these challenges? How we face these, shapes our lives and who we are, ultimately determining what we can create for ourselves.

It's all about resilience. How easy do you find it to get back up again after you've fallen down? How easy is it for you to recover after disappointment, shame, or embarrassment...

Gratitude allows us to look at these situations in a different light and see things from another perspective. We always have a choice in how we perceive our life. We can either choose to wallow in our sorrows and mope around, feeling sorry for ourselves, painting ourselves to be the victim. Or, we can look at things from another angle.

If we do this and realise that life is happening FOR us rather than AGAINST us, then we can make the decision to be grateful for every single thing that happens in our lives.

Have you ever heard that old saying "every cloud has a silver lining'? - it's so true. No matter what life throws at us, we're always able to bounce back from it. At the time that something happens, in that very moment, we're not always in the right frame of mind to see the lessons to be learned, but once we take that deep breath, and look back at the situation, there is ALWAYS a lesson there.

Life's gifts don't always come wrapped in that red, sparkly bow. Sometimes we need space and time to allow us to process the event, and then we can look back and learn.

When we look back at these types of situations, we can see how things actually unravelled and how the tough moments we experienced were actually key parts of that lesson that we were due to learn.

You will grow in life because of your own experiences. You learn, you discover, you grow, and you become.

So going back to today's thought-provoking question, how can I learn from the daily challenges in my life?

Think about a situation in your life right now that you thought hadn't gone as well as you thought it could have. This could be an argument with someone, poor performance of a task you attempted, whatever it is, make it personal to you.

Think of the challenges that you faced, and really delve deep into what happened, picking it apart at the bone. What lessons can you learn from this situation? What is the silver lining in this dark cloud?

When you really dig into this, it'll allow your brain to really have a breakthrough which ultimately will help you to redefine who you are in the face of adversity and challenges. Keep picking at the layers of this onion to get to the root of why things went the way that they did and you'll eventually get to the point of knowing deep down inside that you've got this.

Always remember that there's light at the end of the tunnel and sometimes the challenges in life are just part of our experience here on Earth.

Be curious, reflect, acknowledge, and ask yourself: how can I learn from the daily challenges in my life?

Feel free to take a picture of your daily answers if you're feeling brave enough to share, use the hashtag

#31daysofgratitude, and tag my main account which is @cannycrystals across all social media.

I look forward to seeing you all again tomorrow for day 3.

WHAT IS SOMETHING THAT MADE ME SMILE YESTERDAY?

....

....

....

WHAT CAN I DO TO MAKE MYSELF FEEL GOOD AND LOVE MYSELF TODAY?

....

....

....

WHAT IS ONE THING THAT I'M GRATEFUL FOR TODAY?

....

....

....

HOW CAN I LEARN FROM THE DAILY CHALLENGES IN MY LIFE?

....

....

....

DAY 3

Introducing Self-Love

Welcome to Day 3. Today we're going to look at how gratitude can really inspire you to see the world through a new lens, or with new eyes, from a different perspective and different point of view. Gratitude can really influence and elevate how we look at everything around us.

Are you the kind of person that would see a glass half filled with water as half empty, or half full? Do you always see the brighter side of things in life, or are you immediately drawn to the negatives? Do you see what is missing, or what we have in abundance?

Our perspective, and where we stand looking at each of these situations, creates this viewpoint from which we see each of these circumstances, and we can change this perspective by simply thinking about where we place our focus.

We know fine well from studying things like the Law of Attraction that our thoughts are magnetic, and what we think, we attract more of. So when we place our focus on feelings of gratitude, happiness and joy, we attract more experiences of gratitude, happiness and joy too.

When we wallow in the sadness, despair and scarcity, we're only allowing our minds to look for more experiences like these to prove that these feelings are true.

So we have a choice in life; we can either concentrate on the good, or we can focus on the bad. But whatever we give our attention to, that's what we will attract more of in our lives.

Let's start by looking at ourselves. We all have differing opinions about ourselves. Some are happy and content, some aren't so much, but we all have a definite opinion about who we are, how we act, what kind of a person we are, how successful we are, etc.

This is where we can use gratitude to help each one of us accept who we really are and show ourselves some true compassion and self-love. You might find it a little uncomfortable at first to give yourself all these different compliments, you might feel vain even, but the reality is, the more we start to feel comfortable with who we are deep down inside, the easier it becomes to get out there and attain the life that we really want.

So today, as well as your three daily journal questions, I want you to take 5-10 minutes to write a list, as long as you possibly can about what you love about yourself. This can be anything from you liking the way your hair looks today, to how you dress, even down to your qualities of things like how empathetic you are with people, or how considerate you are of other people's feelings. Whatever it is, whatever you love about YOU, write it down.

Some people will naturally find this really easy, whereas others will find this quite hard to do. And that's fine – that's part of who we are. Just notice how this feels for you, because self-love and self-acceptance is available to us all, to enable us to show up with more confidence in our lives. There are so many aspects of our lives that we can shine a light on and look at to be grateful for.

And that brings us to today's thought-provoking question: what do you love most about yourself?

Give yourself permission to embrace who you really are. This practice will be so empowering for you to become your best self. Make sure to really take the time to feel this gratitude about yourself. Some people even like to hold their hands over their hearts as they read back what they wrote as this helps them to really be grateful for it.

Feel free to take a picture of your daily answers if you're feeling brave enough to share, use the hashtag #31daysofgratitude and tag my main account which is @cannycrystals across all socials.

I look forward to seeing you all again tomorrow for day 4.

WHAT IS SOMETHING THAT MADE ME SMILE YESTERDAY?

....

....

....

WHAT CAN I DO TO MAKE MYSELF FEEL GOOD AND LOVE MYSELF TODAY?

....

....

....

WHAT IS ONE THING THAT I'M GRATEFUL FOR TODAY?

....

....

....

WHAT DO YOU LOVE ABOUT YOURSELF?

....

....

....

DAY 4

Looking at Your Skills

Welcome to day 4. Today we're going to look at your skills. Each of us has a particular skill set in our lives, and we're going to appreciate those skills today.

So what do I mean when I say "skills"? It could be related to expertise, for example, the ability you have to perform well in a certain category or whilst doing a specific task. It's all about using those skills that you've learned over the years to achieve what you want in life.

Your skills are ultimately what help you to get what you desire. So the more that you're grateful for the skillset that you have, the more you're going to grow as a person and gain more positive skills to help you grow even further – it's a catch-22 situation, and you'll develop more and more as time goes on.

Your ability to make a positive impact on the world and everyone around you all lies in the skills you have to radiate gratitude.

The good thing about skills is that we can learn new ones every single day, but we can also learn to hone in on current skills and focus on them, sharpening them and learning to enhance them more and more as time goes on.

Learning a new skill in life can really help guide us down new paths and bring about new opportunities for us all. You know fine well that sometimes in order to progress into a new career or a new job role, you may need to learn a new skill.

So let's look at the skills that you have right now because looking deeper at these gives us a better understanding of the person that we could actually be and who we're becoming.

Skills are something to be thankful for because we can learn new skills and combine them together in really creative ways. Some skills will come to us effortlessly and easily, and some we must learn as we progress along in life. These are the ones that we need to focus our efforts and resilience on to achieve but trust me when I say that they're worth it.

Usually, the path that we go through to hone in on these types of skills, is the ultimate journey for you to learn something along the way. But as I said earlier, our skills make us who we are and totally influence who we are as people.

So today, as well as your 3 standard questions, really take a moment to think about your own skillset. What skills are you thankful for?

Once you've written your list, read back through it and take 5-10 minutes to acknowledge and appreciate all of the things that you are able to do, have and be because of the skillsets that you have mastered over the years, ultimately leading you to where you are today.

Feel free to take a picture of your daily answers if you're feeling brave enough to share, use the hashtag #31daysofgratitude and tag my main account which is @cannycrystals across socials. I look forward to seeing you all again tomorrow for day 5.

WHAT IS SOMETHING THAT MADE ME SMILE YESTERDAY?

....

....

....

WHAT CAN I DO TO MAKE MYSELF FEEL GOOD AND LOVE MYSELF TODAY?

....

....

....

WHAT IS ONE THING THAT I'M GRATEFUL FOR TODAY?

....

....

....

WHAT SKILLS ARE YOU THANKFUL FOR?

....

....

....

DAY 5

Accepting Compliments

Welcome to day 5. Today our focus is going to be on compliments. You might have noticed this in your own daily life, but some people aren't particularly good at taking compliments, me included. If someone said to me something along the lines of "I like your t-shirt" I'd usually respond with something along the lines of "Oh, this old thing? I've had it for years". But why didn't I just say, "Thank you" and accept the compliment?

We as human beings tend to be more accepting of an insult than a compliment, and when people do say nice things to us unless you're a master of self-acceptance, it can really leave us baffled. Why is that? Why do we feel those feelings of embarrassment, awkwardness, and confusion when we receive a compliment?

When we don't value the thing that we're being complimented on, we can easily become dismissive of the compliment itself, and push it back to them. Sometimes we can even question why that person has given us the compliment in the first place! What do they really want? What's the underlying reason they've given us this compliment? What are they fishing for?

But think of it like this – if we can't receive compliments, and be accepting of these, how can we fully embrace external feedback? Can you open your heart and allow this inside? Because if you can, then you're able to let in all the good things that others see about you, hear about you, and perceive about you!

Compliments can therefore really prove to you that you are valued, loved, and appreciated by those surrounding you. So, although you might not think that compliments are relevant to gratitude, I'm here to tell you that they are... MASSIVELY!

Just like good intentions, compliments show us how other people are perceiving us on a day-to-day basis. We all have blind spots within our lives, areas within us that we never shine a light on. This may be something simple such as being a good listener. We might not see this in ourselves, but when someone gives us that compliment of "you're a really good listener!" that would really make us think, and eventually bring us to realise that skill inside of us.

These compliments may show us all the values within us that we undermine. All the things that other people love, respect and value about us that we tend to just brush off.

Compliments ultimately bring about self-love and self-worth because they allow you to see what the other person saw in you, through their eyes. Isn't that a great tool to have at your disposal? Someone likes your hair today; to you, you may be thinking, "Jesus Christ, I got ready in such a rush this morning, how can anyone possibly give me a compliment about my hair?" but take a moment to see things from their perspective. They may not have been able to afford a fancy hairdryer, or straighteners, or even hot water to wash their hair. Compliments, therefore, are the harbinger of gratitude and happiness.

We can use compliments to deepen our own sense of self-love and self-acceptance. We'll start to value them more and more as time goes on because they can really help us deepen our gratitude.

So grab your pen, and answer your 3 questions:
- What is something that made me smile yesterday?
- What can I do to make myself feel good and love myself today? And...
- What is 1 thing that I'm grateful for today?

Today's task is all around compliments and stepping out of your comfort zone. I want you to write down any compliments that you receive today or any that you've received in the past, and write down how they made you feel inside.

It's ok to write down that they made you feel uneasy, or uncomfortable, or awkward. Write down how you responded to that compliment; did you brush it off? Did you accept it? Did you say thank you, or did you play it down?

How are you able to use that compliment to look inside of yourself at an area that you're not currently shining a light on? Are you able to say thank you?

Receiving compliments is ultimately strengthening how you receive things in life. So the more you're open to receive, and feel good through receiving, you're allowing yourself and opening yourself up to receive even more.

Just as a little added challenge here, either today, or whenever you're next around another person, drop them a genuine compliment. Don't say something ingenuine, really look inside that person and offer them a compliment. It might just be their hair or their clothes, but it may be a value or skill that person has that you're appreciative of. Whatever it is, take note of how your compliment hits with that other person and how they either accept or reject it.

The more we learn from each other, the more we learn about ourselves.

Feel free to take a picture of your daily answers if you're feeling brave enough to share, use the hashtag #31daysofgratitude and tag my main account which is @cannycrystals across all socials.

I look forward to seeing you all again tomorrow for day 6.

WHAT IS SOMETHING THAT MADE ME SMILE YESTERDAY?

....

....

....

WHAT CAN I DO TO MAKE MYSELF FEEL GOOD AND LOVE MYSELF TODAY?

....

....

....

WHAT IS ONE THING THAT I'M GRATEFUL FOR TODAY?

....

....

....

WHAT COMPLIMENTS DID YOU RECEIVE TODAY?

....

....

....

DAY 6

Affirmative Statements

Welcome to Day 6. Today is all about using affirmations and affirmative statements to enhance the gratitude already inside of you.

Affirmations are simple statements read out in the first person, in the present tense, allowing your mind to take them in as truth. They can help you to challenge and overcome self-sabotaging and negative thoughts, and when you repeat them often and believe in them, you can start to make positive changes.

You might consider affirmations to be unrealistic and pass them off as "wishful thinking" but try looking at positive affirmations this way: many of us do repetitive exercises to improve our physical health, and affirmations are basically like exercises for our mind and outlook.

These positive mental repetitions can reprogram our thinking patterns so that, over time, we begin to think, and act, differently. For example, evidence suggests that affirmations can help you to perform better at work. According to researchers, spending just a few minutes thinking about your best qualities before a high-pressure meeting, can really calm your nerves, increase your confidence, and improve your chances of a more successful outcome.

An affirmation of gratitude is a way for you to start and end every day on a positive note. If you take a few minutes every day to simply write out what you're grateful for when you go to sleep at night, you'll not only go to bed thinking grateful thoughts but also wake up starting them.

Because your emotions are fuelled by your thoughts, this is going to translate your thoughts about gratefulness into happy emotions. This is going to elevate your mood, provide you with energy, and improve your outlook on life.

There are a few ways that you can use affirmations in your life. You can use positive affirmations to remind yourself of what you have to be thankful for in life, they can be used to keep yourself grounded, and can also be used to keep negative and unhelpful thoughts at bay.

So for today's practice, we're going to answer our 3 main questions, which are also on the following pages:
- What is something that made me smile yesterday?
- What can I do to make myself feel good and love myself today? And...
- What is 1 thing that I'm grateful for today?

And then we're going to repeat 5 affirmative statements whenever we can. Those statements are as follows:

"I live in a state of gratitude, and I am always thankful for the help and support of others who have helped me along the way."

"When I work for something, I tend to achieve it. Therefore, I am appreciative of the results, and I value the work I put in on a daily basis."

"While my thoughts might vary from day to day, my giving of thanks extends far beyond what I think about daily. My grateful spirit is present in each step and action that I take."

"While I might not say it every day, I am always grateful for the love I receive. I try to give love to the best of my

ability, and I am grateful for the love I have yet to receive."

"I am so happy and grateful for everything that I receive. While I might focus on the material things, I know that there is more to life than this. I am grateful for all of it."

The more we repeat this and truly believe it, the more these statements will become living truths in our daily lives. For added effect, you can replay these statements and write them down, repeating them daily for the remainder of the 31 days whilst standing looking at yourself in a mirror.

I often find added power in repeating affirmations to myself whilst staring into my own eyes in my reflection. It helps me believe them more as gospel and truth.

Feel free to take a picture of your daily answers if you're feeling brave enough to share, use the hashtag #31daysofgratitude and tag my main account which is @cannycrystals across all socials.

I look forward to seeing you all again tomorrow for day 7.

WHAT IS SOMETHING THAT MADE ME SMILE YESTERDAY?

....

....

....

WHAT CAN I DO TO MAKE MYSELF FEEL GOOD AND LOVE MYSELF TODAY?

....

....

....

WHAT IS ONE THING THAT I'M GRATEFUL FOR TODAY?

....

....

....

Day 7

Experiences of Gratitude

Welcome back to Day 7. If you've made it this far, well done, really! A big round of applause from me. That's 7 consecutive days that you've done a little practice around gratitude. That's a big milestone. The more we do something, the more it's engrained within us and we're more likely to keep it up, so well done so far.

Just take a few moments to acknowledge that win, because it *is* a win. Thank yourself for showing up, and thank yourself for taking the time out to commit to yourself and develop yourself more and more spiritually every single day.

When we appreciate the small things in life, like this little win, we immediately open the floodgates to more similar experiences of abundance and gratitude entering our lives.

Today's episode is all about experiences of gratitude, and I'd like to begin just by defining exactly what I mean by that. So, this could be an event, a day, or a moment in time that made you feel something, just a general experience that left a big imprint on your mind.

It might be a momentous occasion like getting your first house, getting married, having a child, the first day of college, a first date, gaining a promotion... whatever it is, it's something that's shifted you in some way, shape or form as a person.

When I think about experiences in my life, I'm immediately drawn to milestone key events like the day our mortgage went through, my first date with my partner, the day he proposed to me, and the day I got my dog, JJ.

But experiences aren't always happy ones – and in fact when I look back at the last 3 years, one of the biggest things that happened to me was that I lost my Granda. He wasn't ill or anything. He died suddenly, and nobody got the chance to say goodbye. And although this experience is far from a happy one for me, I can still find gratitude within it.

I can still be happy and grateful for being able to experience the last 32 years by his side as the Father figure in my life. I can be grateful that every single other experience I had in my life was fully supported by him and his love. I can be grateful that he shaped me into whom I am today by teaching me the life lessons I needed.

Experiences, no matter good or bad, will test our courage and resilience. They will ultimately shape who we are. They will all teach us something that we need to know to be able to move forward in life, and that's why it's worthwhile acknowledging experiences that happen to us throughout our time here on Earth.

So today, as well as answering your 3 journal questions, I also want you to take a moment to think about a specific experience that you are thankful for. It could be a good or bad experience, your choice, but I want you to really describe the experience and journal about why this was so significant and meaningful for you in your journey to where you are today.

So answer this question: what experience has helped shape me into the person that I am today and what did I learn from this?

Feel free to take a picture of your daily answers if you're feeling brave enough to share, use the hashtag #31daysofgratitude and tag my main account which is @cannycrystals across all socials.

I look forward to seeing you all again tomorrow for day 8.

WHAT IS SOMETHING THAT MADE ME SMILE YESTERDAY?

....
....
....

WHAT CAN I DO TO MAKE MYSELF FEEL GOOD AND LOVE MYSELF TODAY?

....
....
....

WHAT IS ONE THING THAT I'M GRATEFUL FOR TODAY?

....
....
....

WHAT EXPERIENCE HAS HELPED SHAPE ME INTO THE PERSON THAT I AM TODAY AND WHAT DID I LEARN FROM THIS?

....
....
....

DAY 8
Gratitude for Challenges

Welcome back to day 8. The start of the second week in the 31 Days of Gratitude.

Today is all about challenges. Every single one of us encounters some form of challenge in our everyday lives. Sometimes they make us stop and think about what's just happened, sometimes they stop us completely.

Whatever happens though, we always find a way to navigate through it and overcome these circumstances. Remember what I said on Day 2; the lessons that we learn through this process really help to shape who we are, who we need to be, and what we do in life.

When things do happen to us though, the first thing we do is wish that it wasn't there, because who wants to be inconvenienced in life at the end of the day? We all want an easier life, and the ideal road for all of us is one that's easy and smooth to navigate.

However, once we're through the eye of the storm and heading out the other side of it all, we often look back in hindsight and realise what a great gift that challenge actually was to us.

A few years ago when my Granda passed, the months that followed were excruciating. I just wanted them to be over and I couldn't see any form of positives to come out of that experience. At the end of the day, it's a death — what possible positives could come out of that?

But now, years later, whilst working with my life coach, she mentioned that his passing was his gift to me and that nothing in my life right now, including my business, Canny Crystals, would have even existed had I not gone down that path looking for comfort through crystals. In fact, come to think of it, I probably would still be working for the NHS right now.

That dark path lead me down my journey of spiritual and self-development, which ultimately lead me to where I am today.

Through reflection, we can all look back at circumstances within our lives and take some form of positive from any negative situation. We can choose what something meant, and reflect on how that inspired, shaped and affected us.

When we choose to see how a challenge helped us to grow, our eyes are opened for us and we can see the bigger picture. We can view each circumstance with gratitude, benefits and just generally knowing that we wouldn't be who we are today if those experiences hadn't happened to us.

Life's challenges aren't meant to paralyse us, they're meant to help us discover who we really are.

So you know by now that each day we're going to answer our 3 main questions, which are also in the show notes for this episode:
- What is something that made me smile yesterday?
- What can I do to make myself feel good and love myself today? And...
- What is 1 thing that I'm grateful for today?

But I also want you to answer the following too: what did I learn from a life-changing challenge in my life?

I want you to think about something that happened to you in your past. Something that you thought had totally paralysed you and that you saw as a massive challenge. Something that you are grateful for and you're actually happy that you got to experience.

Take a moment to reflect on that moment. You might want to sit and close your eyes, you may even want to take yourself to a quiet room and light a candle, you could even do this in the bath... somewhere you're not going to be disturbed.

Really feel that sense of gratitude to appreciate who you became because of that particular challenge. It may have been that a family member passed, like my story, or it may be that someone delivered you some life-changing news, or you had a car accident, or you ended up in hospital because of something... whatever it is, what could you learn from that, and how has that shaped who you are today?

Really dig deep with this one. Did you learn new skills? Did it make you a stronger person? Did it change the way you perceive certain situations?

Feel free to take a picture of your daily answers if you're feeling brave enough to share, use the hashtag #31daysofgratitude and tag my main account which is @cannycrystals across all socials.

I look forward to seeing you all again tomorrow for day 9.

WHAT IS SOMETHING THAT MADE ME SMILE YESTERDAY?

....

....

....

WHAT CAN I DO TO MAKE MYSELF FEEL GOOD AND LOVE MYSELF TODAY?

....

....

....

WHAT IS ONE THING THAT I'M GRATEFUL FOR TODAY?

....

....

....

WHAT DID I LEARN FROM A LIFE-CHANGING CHALLENGE IN MY LIFE?

....

....

....

DAY 9

Money Doesn't Buy Gratitude

Welcome back to day 9 of the 31 Days of Gratitude. Today we're going to look at a powerful mindset that can really spark those feelings of joy and happiness in an instant.

We know fine well that if we buy experiences such as holidays, or nights away, or we've bought the dream car, or we just treat ourselves to something nice, we're almost compelled to stop and look at how lucky we are to have these in our lives.

However, if we only feel grateful for these types of things in life, the big things, we miss out on the smaller experiences, all the everyday moments. There's a famous quote, I'm not sure who it's by but it says, "Be grateful for the little things because one day we might look back and realise that these were actually the big things".

We need to really make time in our hectic lives to sit in that gratitude for the everyday things that happen to us. Not just the things that we spend our money on, but the free experiences we have in life every single day.

Sometimes it feels like life just happens to us and that we need to get from A to B, not taking notice of the journey in between. Life can get busy, and in that rush, we tend to normalise the things around us that actually, when we stop to think about it, are incredible. We just need to take two moments to recognise them and feel super grateful for them.

Gratitude is a real skill that can make you feel satisfied, happy, and filled up from the inside out. So wouldn't it be amazing if we could feel like this more often without spending money on large experiences, materialistic gifts to ourselves and buying things just to make us feel better about life?

Imagine if we could get that same buzz about waking up on a morning and realising we're alive another day, or looking at the sunrise and realising how beautifully natural it is and that it happens every single day, or maybe just a gorgeous smile from someone that you live with, or the fact you can have a conversation with them.

Life happens in the moment. Life happens in the here and now. When we realise this, and we realise that we can find joy in the simplest of things, we unlock sheer happiness within our bodies. This ultimately helps us to manifest things we want in life because we can see the sheer abundance that surrounds every part of our lives, every single day. We just usually overlook these smaller experiences because we're too busy looking out for the larger things.

So today we're going to answer our 3 main questions,
- What is something that made me smile yesterday?
- What can I do to make myself feel good and love myself today? And...
- What is 1 thing that I'm grateful for today?

But I also want you to think about experiences to be grateful for that we haven't spent money on. This can be anything from breathing to something that you received from another person. There are SO many things that bring sheer joy and appreciation in life that we don't require money for.

So answer this question: what small things in life am I grateful for that don't cost me a thing?

When we really put our all into this and think about the gratitude that follows, we feel the abundance that surrounds us that is free to us every single day.

By doing this exercise, it'll allow us to reprogramme our minds and start to appreciate the littlest things that we would usually skip over. I want you to really focus on them and feel those feelings inside of your body, on how good that feels to you.

Have you ever been for a walk in nature, and really taken in your surroundings? Maybe it was in a forest, or by a lake, or in a park, wherever it was, you know how good that feels when you notice things rather than walking by them with your head in your phone. You feel like you've accomplished something. Just allow yourself the time to stop and pause at certain points throughout your day. See what is present, and this will help you find joy and gratitude in all of the things that money can't buy you.

Using mindfulness can really help you to focus on this. Mindfulness is all about living life in the present moment. If you live in the past, you will often suffer from depression. If you live in the future, you will often suffer from anxiety. But when you live in the present moment, you're free of these symptoms and you can see life for exactly what it is in the here and now.

Feel free to take a picture of your daily answers if you're feeling brave enough to share, use the hashtag #31daysofgratitude and tag my main account which is @cannycrystals across all socials.

I look forward to seeing you all again tomorrow for day 10.

WHAT IS SOMETHING THAT MADE ME SMILE YESTERDAY?

....

....

....

WHAT CAN I DO TO MAKE MYSELF FEEL GOOD AND LOVE MYSELF TODAY?

....

....

....

WHAT IS ONE THING THAT I'M GRATEFUL FOR TODAY?

....

....

....

WHAT SMALL THINGS AM I GRATEFUL FOR THAT DON'T COST A THING?

....

....

....

DAY 10
Making Changes in Your Life

Welcome back to day 10, where we're now almost a third of the way through this 31-day process. So let's just take a quick moment to reflect and give thanks that you've made it this far and that you're willing to do what's needed to make that change in your life.

If you carry on with this for the next 3 weeks, you're more likely to continue seeing circumstances in life to be grateful for, giving you more joy, satisfaction, and contentment.

When we look at small changes like this at that moment in time, we can severely underestimate how significant they are, but over time, these small changes can severely snowball and ultimately create your dream life before you even know it. Circumstances will feel different for you, experiences will show up differently for you, and life will appear different – in a good way.

We all crave change at some point in our lives. You might think, no I don't, I hate change. But change is what sees us through transformation and development. It invites us to step up and try new things. This is exactly why we keep changing our dreams, goals, and vision to get where we want to be. There's a part of us that deep down knows that change is good for us.

Change helps us to develop new skills and new abilities - we can expand our comfort zone and are able to hold more of what life has to offer. Change is 100% something to be grateful for.

Change can be hard to accept at first, but the more you think about it, change can invite you into new experiences, new stepping stones into new circumstances... It can really evolve you through these new experiences into the person you're due to become.

These new experiences help and allow us to see life in a different light. Something that we've done day in day out for years could seem like a totally new experience for example. It can really help to transform our future, just by allowing and accepting that change.

So today we're going to answer our 3 main questions,
- What is something that made me smile yesterday?
- What can I do to make myself feel good and love myself today? And...
- What is 1 thing that I'm grateful for today?

But I also want you to answer the following: what change in your life has happened in the last few years that you are truly grateful for? Really think about what that change was, how it affected you, how it affected your everyday life, and how it affected how you appear to other people. Write it all down, and journal it all out.

What did that change look like, and how did it evolve you to where you are today?

Feel free to take a picture of your daily answers if you're feeling brave enough to share, use the hashtag #31daysofgratitude and tag my main account which is @cannycrystals across all socials.

I look forward to seeing you all again tomorrow for day 11.

WHAT IS SOMETHING THAT MADE ME SMILE YESTERDAY?

....

....

....

WHAT CAN I DO TO MAKE MYSELF FEEL GOOD AND LOVE MYSELF TODAY?

....

....

....

WHAT IS ONE THING THAT I'M GRATEFUL FOR TODAY?

....

....

....

WHAT CHANGE IN YOUR LIFE HAS HAPPENED IN THE LAST FEW YEARS THAT YOU ARE TRULY GRATEFUL FOR?

....

....

....

DAY 11

Strengths Inside of You

Welcome back to day 11. Today's challenge will really help you to have a greater sense of appreciation for who you are as a person, as we're going to be taking a look into our strengths and what we're grateful for in that aspect.

We're going to delve deep into all the strengths that we possess and those strengths that make us who we are, which enable us to show up in the world as the people that we are.

Using our strengths, we can identify the areas in our lives that require a little bit of added help and support, and we can also use them to know where we're best placed to get better results out of our day-to-day activities.

Knowing what your strengths are, allows you to focus on all the things that you're capable of and all the things that you enjoy.

So what do I mean when I say your strengths? I mean your capabilities and your qualities that help you with your success in life. In terms of qualities, these could be things like resilience, passion, or commitment to a task at hand. In terms of capabilities, these could be things like your creativity, your ideas, or your problem-solving skills.

We all have things like this inside of us, strengths in every single one of us, that help to empower us, and today is all about acknowledging what this means to you personally.

We're going to really shine a light here on the things that you're great at and to not shy away from it, but really look into what strengths help you live the best possible version of yourself.

Using our strengths, we're able to fully own ourselves and know that because of things we're good at, we're able to create the life we desire.

Using affirmations, we're all empowered when we say things like "I can do this" or "I can have this", and when we're grateful for all the things we're able to do because of our strengths, we become truly appreciative of them. Strengths can truly transform how we're able to work with other people, how we can create loving relationships and friendships, and how we can redefine our sense of ourselves.

So today, we're going to answer our 3 main questions,
- What is something that made me smile yesterday?
- What can I do to make myself feel good and love myself today? And...
- What is 1 thing that I'm grateful for today?

And then once you've answered these, I want you to sit back and meditate for 5 minutes, just really get into the present moment following your breath, and then ask yourself: what strength of yours are you truly grateful for? And you can really expand on your answer by thinking in detail about WHY you're grateful for it.

It could be something as simple as being grateful for your listening strengths, which allow you to deepen your relationships and friendship by being able to offer our help and advice to others, or it may be that you're grateful for your problem-solving strength which allows you to overcome most obstacles that you're faced with by thinking logistically about them and how you're going to get by.

You could even journal right away about how this strength came about for you – did you learn it? Were you born with it? Was it something that rubbed off on you from another person?

Look at your entire life as a whole, and really feel grateful for those strengths that you've learned, owned and cultivated over the years.

Feel free to take a picture of your daily answers if you're feeling brave enough to share, use the hashtag #31daysofgratitude and tag my main account which is @cannycrystals across all socials.

I look forward to seeing you all again tomorrow for day 12.

WHAT IS SOMETHING THAT MADE ME SMILE YESTERDAY?

....

....

....

WHAT CAN I DO TO MAKE MYSELF FEEL GOOD AND LOVE MYSELF TODAY?

....

....

....

WHAT IS ONE THING THAT I'M GRATEFUL FOR TODAY?

....

....

....

WHAT STRENGTH OF YOURS ARE YOU TRULY GRATEFUL FOR?

....

....

....

DAY 12

Being Grateful for Failures

Welcome back to day 12. Today, we're going to look at the failures that have occurred in your life. We're not going to dwell on the negatives however, we're going to look at failure through the lens of gratitude.

I hope that by the time we get to the end of today's practice, you're going to feel inspired and empowered to look at failure in a brand new light, that actually enables you to explore life as your best possible self.

You know as well as I do, we can't succeed all the time. Sooner or later, we experience failure in our lives for a number of reasons. This will happen multiple times; sometimes failures are small, and sometimes they're huge.

If you're sitting there right now listening to this thinking that you've never failed at anything, that's more than likely an indication that you've not properly stepped out of your comfort zone. You've always played it safe.

Nobody likes to or wants to fail – in fact, we as human beings don't like to be seen as a failure. We don't want to be judged, criticised, or rejected for being a failure. We really fear getting things in life wrong.

Failure can really knock down our confidence, self-esteem, and worthiness. Especially when we have real-life examples from the past that this is true. But with all things, it's really easy to just accept failure and beat ourselves up over it.

Hindsight is a wonderful thing, and looking back at past experiences we can see clearly how to have avoided failure in the first place. Unfortunately, this is normal. We all learn something in the process of failing, and we all learn how not to do that thing again and make the same mistake twice.

Failure can be emotionally triggering and painful inside. It can really inhibit our sense of identity. Even when we know deep down inside that we can learn from failure and understand that it can help us grow.

Our relationship with failure is usually a negative one, so can you really allow failure to become a part of your life? Can you create an opening or a space, where you're willing to take a risk, because you know and understand that even if you do, and it doesn't work out, you'll have learned something from that particular experience?

So today, we're going to answer our 3 main questions,
- What is something that made me smile yesterday?
- What can I do to make myself feel good and love myself today? And...
- What is 1 thing that I'm grateful for today?

And then once you've answered these, I want you to ask yourself: what failure have you experienced in your life that you've learned a valuable lesson from and are grateful for failing?

We can really learn to take that lesson, knowledge and understanding from the failure incident. The more times that we learn from things like this, and the more that we actually grow, the easier it becomes to be comfortable when inevitably failure does show up in your life.

By intentionally and purposefully changing our relationship by applying the gratitude process over the top and sugar-coating what's actually happening, we can become the best possible version of ourselves.

Enjoy today's lesson writing about your past failures. Make sure you journal down examples of past failures that you're now grateful and thankful for because ultimately, they're what's shaped you into the person that you are today.

Feel free to take a picture of your daily answers if you're feeling brave enough to share, use the hashtag #31daysofgratitude and tag my main account which is @cannycrystals across all socials.

I look forward to seeing you all again tomorrow for day 13.

WHAT IS SOMETHING THAT MADE ME SMILE YESTERDAY?

....

....

....

WHAT CAN I DO TO MAKE MYSELF FEEL GOOD AND LOVE MYSELF TODAY?

....

....

....

WHAT IS ONE THING THAT I'M GRATEFUL FOR TODAY?

....

....

....

WHAT FAILURE HAVE YOU EXPERIENCED IN LIFE THAT YOU'VE LEARNED A VALUABLE LESSON FROM?

....

....

....

DAY 13

Achievements to be Grateful For

Welcome back to day 13. Today, we're going to look at the achievements that we've made in our lives.

So what do I mean when I say "achievements"? Achievements in life are successes you've attained, particularly those that you're proud of. For example, when someone asks you about your achievements in a job interview, they're asking you to share experiences that you consider impressive or times that you've proven your capabilities or something that's helped you develop in an ideal direction.

What you consider an achievement may differ from what others think, but there are often common traits that achievements share, such as:

- A problem that you addressed
- A challenging process
- A realisation of your values or goals, or even
- A change in your condition or outlook

Whatever you've overcome in life, these are your achievements. And they're different for every single person.

If I sat you down and asked you, what's your greatest achievement, what would you say? Maybe it would be having a child, settling down with your significant other and raising a family, or maybe you'd tell me that you created a business from the ground up with little to no help, and now this business supports you and your family's lifestyle.

Whatever it is, give it some thought today and really shine a light on that achievement. In fact, why stop at just one thing? Today we're going to list 3 of our main achievements in life.

So today, we're going to answer our 3 main questions,
- What is something that made me smile yesterday?
- What can I do to make myself feel good and love myself today? And...
- What is 1 thing that I'm grateful for today?

And then once you've answered these, I want you to ask yourself: what 3 things have you achieved in your life that you're super proud of? List each one and as you do, think back to how you felt when you reached those achievements.

Did they make you happy? Excited? Hyper? Who did you tell when you reached them? Re-live those moments inside and really feel that gratitude and positive energy bubbling up inside of you.

Feel free to take a picture of your daily answers if you're feeling brave enough to share, use the hashtag #31daysofgratitude and tag my main account which is @cannycrystals across all socials.

I look forward to seeing you all again tomorrow for day 14.

WHAT IS SOMETHING THAT MADE ME SMILE YESTERDAY?

....

....

....

WHAT CAN I DO TO MAKE MYSELF FEEL GOOD AND LOVE MYSELF TODAY?

....

....

....

WHAT IS ONE THING THAT I'M GRATEFUL FOR TODAY?

....

....

....

WHAT 3 THINGS HAVE YOU ACHIEVED IN LIFE THAT YOU'RE SUPER PROUD OF?

....

....

....

DAY 14

Living in the Present Moment

Welcome back to day 14 and another dose of gratitude to start your morning. Today we're going to look at living in the present moment and using gratitude to see what we have right now, even though we may just be lying in bed reading this, sitting at a desk, or on our way to work, or whatever it is. By the end of today's episode, you're going to be able to show gratitude for whatever it is that you're doing right now.

Mindfulness is a tool and technique for looking at the present moment. It's said that when a person lives in the past, they tend to deal with depression because they can't stop thinking about all the things that could have been. When a person lives in the future, they tend to deal with anxiety, because they can't stop thinking about all the different things that could happen and go wrong.

But when we live in the present moment, in the here and now, we don't fear the future or the past, and our minds are able to focus on other things instead.

When we are distracted, distant and not fully immersed in the here and now, nothing is ever enough - we often feel we need more to be complete. We never actually feel satisfied.

When we make gratitude the essence of each present moment, abundance multiplies. Simply being present and being grateful creates the wholeness and completeness that is ultimately what some people refer to as "grace". It is by expressing these things that we align ourselves with the Universe.

Gratitude enriches the present moment – bringing it to life. Grace can only be found in the present moment, and it lives in the here and now. You know when you feel alive, and you get that buzz inside of you, say for example when you go to a theme park and go on a rollercoaster, that's because you're living in the present moment. As you go over those huge dips on the rollercoaster track, you're not sitting there worrying about something that happened last week, or something that could potentially harm you in 5 years' time... if you're like me, the only thought going through your head is "please don't let me fall out of this!".

Being present has become a challenge that we all face right now. Life is full of distractions including things like the news, media, social media, mobile phones, etc. Being grateful in the present moment shifts our attention away from what seems to be missing. It begins to erase old anxious habits and empty desires. We find completeness in the present moment because that's the only place it can ever be found.

So today, we're going to answer our 3 main questions,
- What is something that made me smile yesterday?
- What can I do to make myself feel good and love myself today? And...
- What is 1 thing that I'm grateful for today?

And then once you've answered these, I want you to do a little visualisation. Close your eyes and centre yourself. Imagine the perfect day at the beach. See the sun shining on the water. Feel the sand between your toes. Hear the seagulls flying above you, and the chatter of other families around you. And after about 60 seconds of visualising this scene, you can then open your eyes. You'll find that the room that you're in right now seems a little brighter than normal. This is what every present moment should feel like.

So ask yourself today: as I sit where I am right now, what am I grateful for right now in this present moment? And just to clarify, I want you to think of a different answer than the one you used for the "What is 1 thing that I'm grateful for today" question.

I want you to feel any feelings that come up internally for you when you think of that thing.

Feel free to take a picture of your daily answers if you're feeling brave enough to share, use the hashtag #31daysofgratitude and tag my main account which is @cannycrystals across all socials.

I look forward to seeing you all again tomorrow for day 15.

WHAT IS SOMETHING THAT MADE ME SMILE YESTERDAY?

....

....

....

WHAT CAN I DO TO MAKE MYSELF FEEL GOOD AND LOVE MYSELF TODAY?

....

....

....

WHAT IS ONE THING THAT I'M GRATEFUL FOR TODAY?

....

....

....

WHAT AM I GRATEFUL FOR RIGHT NOW IN THIS PRESENT MOMENT?

....

....

....

DAY 15

Being Grateful for the Future

Welcome back to day 15 of this 31-day challenge. We're almost halfway and I'm so proud of you if you're still on track doing this challenge day in, day out - so well done!

Today we're going to look at pre-empting the day ahead and the subsequent events that may unfold.

If we worry about something that's coming up, for example, an exciting but worrying meeting at work, we know that although excited about it, the worry will usually get the better of us and rule our morning until this meeting actually goes ahead. Sometimes this can leave people feeling ill and the worry really sets in.

But what if we had control over this? And I'm here to tell you today that you do. You can set your day up to turn out exactly how you want it to go, by giving your focus and attention to it.

Some families, especially those in America, will say "grace" and give their thanks before eating family meals together. They're pre-empting that the meal is going to be amazing, as well as offering their thanks for how that meal was prepared and got onto their table in the first place. So see today's exercise as exactly this... saying "grace" for the day ahead.

So today, we're going to answer our 3 main questions,
- What is something that made me smile yesterday?
- What can I do to make myself feel good and love myself today? And...
- What is 1 thing that I'm grateful for today?

And then once you've answered these, I want you to ask yourself: how is my day going to go today? Really list out every single detail of how you want today to go. What have you got coming up, a meeting, work, a relaxing day, seeing family or friends? Whatever it is, visualise everything going in your favour and really feel the gratitude that today will go your way.

Most of the time you will see and experience the outcome you asked for, and occasionally you won't even know how you benefited from an unexpected event. But when you ask for this outcome and feel sincerely grateful for it, you are using the mathematical Law of Attraction, and you must receive this outcome back, somewhere, at some time.

Whenever you find yourself thinking that chance is at play with something in your life, or think you have no control over something, or when you find yourself hoping something will turn out well, remember that there's no chance when it comes to the law of attraction — you will get what you're thinking and feeling.

Gratitude will help protect you from attracting what you don't want, all the bad outcomes, and it will instead ensure that you get what you do want, the outcomes of an incredible day!

Feel free to take a picture of your daily answers if you're feeling brave enough to share, use the hashtag #31daysofgratitude and tag my main account which is @cannycrystals across all socials.

I look forward to seeing you all again tomorrow for day 16.

WHAT IS SOMETHING THAT MADE ME SMILE YESTERDAY?

....

....

....

WHAT CAN I DO TO MAKE MYSELF FEEL GOOD AND LOVE MYSELF TODAY?

....

....

....

WHAT IS ONE THING THAT I'M GRATEFUL FOR TODAY?

....

....

....

HOW IS MY DAY GOING TO GO TODAY?

....

....

....

DAY 16
Grateful for the Memories

Welcome to day 16, and we're now officially over the halfway mark. By now, you'll have really started to engrain gratitude into your daily life and really have your eyes opened to all the things you've got to be grateful for emotionally. So for the remainder of the challenge, we're going to look at physical things starting with today's task of looking at an old photograph.

I know we don't all have such things as physical photo albums anymore, and that's fine, you can do this on your phone, tablet, or wherever you store your digital photos.

So today, we're going to answer our 3 main questions,
- What is something that made me smile yesterday?
- What can I do to make myself feel good and love myself today? And...
- What is 1 thing that I'm grateful for today?

And then once you've answered these, I want you to grab your device and scroll back to one of the very first photos that you have stored. It could be that you took a photo of your dog lying asleep, or it might be the view from a walk that you were on, or it could even be a photo of a friend on a night out, or a photo of your desk at work.

Whatever photo you choose to work with today, this is the photo I want you to cast your mind back to. Put yourself in the shoes of the past you that took this photo. How did you feel that day, what emotions were you feeling, and what kind of person were you back then?

Really get into the frame of mind of that past version of you. And once you're there, think about what you had to be grateful for at that moment when taking that photo.

So for example, if it's a photo of a view whilst on a walk, you might have just taken the photo because it looked nice, but looking back in hindsight you could be so grateful for the scenery, the friends you were with, the fact you were in such a beautiful environment, the weather, the fact you were so carefree.

Whatever it is, write down in your notebook, what was I grateful for in that photographic moment?

Feel free to take a picture of your daily answers if you're feeling brave enough to share, use the hashtag #31daysofgratitude and tag my main account which is @cannycrystals across all socials.

I look forward to seeing you all again tomorrow for day 17.

WHAT IS SOMETHING THAT MADE ME SMILE YESTERDAY?

....

....

....

WHAT CAN I DO TO MAKE MYSELF FEEL GOOD AND LOVE MYSELF TODAY?

....

....

....

WHAT IS ONE THING THAT I'M GRATEFUL FOR TODAY?

....

....

....

WHAT WAS I GRATEFUL FOR IN THAT PHOTOGRAPHIC MOMENT?

....

....

....

DAY 17

The Air That We Breathe

Welcome back to day 17 and the next chapter in this 31-day challenge. We've got just 2 weeks together remaining until we reach the end. Today I want to continue with some of the physical things we can be grateful for, and today in particular I'm talking about oxygen; O2, the air which surrounds us.

So many of us sit there writing our gratitude lists on a morning thinking of things to be grateful for and really struggle when the one thing that's keeping us alive is invisible, but we're utilising it every minute that we're living.

And I get it, if someone said to me years ago that I should be grateful for the oxygen I breathe, I'd probably have turned to them and thought they were barking mad. Why on Earth should I be grateful for something that is so abundant in life? Isn't that a given?

But in the last 3 years especially, when writing my gratitude lists, I've started to include things that I probably wouldn't have before – and that includes the air that we breathe. Let's face it, without air, we wouldn't exist. If all the air from the world was vacuumed out into space, nothing on this planet would exist. Surely that in itself is something to be grateful for. The air that we breathe keeps us and everything around us alive.

We take one breath after another without giving it any thought, even in our sleep. As we breathe, oxygen feeds every single one of the organs in our bodies.

So today, we're going to answer our 3 main questions,

- What is something that made me smile yesterday?
- What can I do to make myself feel good and love myself today? And...
- What is 1 thing that I'm grateful for today?

And then once you've answered these, I want you to head to a window, or a door, or somewhere you feel like you're partially outdoors, and I just want you to close your eyes, obviously don't do this whilst driving, but close your eyes and take 10 deep breaths in, hold at the top, and out again very slowly. It should take you just over 1 minute to do and will really help to reset your body into the frame of mind of feeling grateful for the air that you take in even when you're unaware of your body doing it on autopilot.

Once you've taken these 10 amazingly deep breaths, look upwards and say out loud "Thank you". Without the air that we breathe, we wouldn't be here today. You can come back to this little task and do it several times throughout the day if you feel like it, or you can just do it once.

Just remember after the last breath to say aloud the magic words, "Thank you". I've even started to incorporate this little task into my morning routine – and you can too if you feel like it. It's a short exercise, but really helps you focus on the smallest things to be grateful for.

Feel free to take a picture of your daily answers if you're feeling brave enough to share, use the hashtag #31daysofgratitude and tag my main account which is @cannycrystals across all socials.

I look forward to seeing you all again tomorrow for day 18.

WHAT IS SOMETHING THAT MADE ME SMILE YESTERDAY?

....

....

....

WHAT CAN I DO TO MAKE MYSELF FEEL GOOD AND LOVE MYSELF TODAY?

....

....

....

WHAT IS ONE THING THAT I'M GRATEFUL FOR TODAY?

....

....

....

DAY 18

Problem-Solving with Gratitude

Welcome back to day 18 of the 31 Days of Gratitude challenge. Today we're going to be looking at giving gratitude for important things in our lives that we need to problem-solve on a daily basis.

Many of us feel like we don't have time in the day to do what we want to do. Some of us have childcare commitments, some of us have elderly family members to look after, some of us have our own businesses and work most of our days... We all have our own problems; we just don't all have the luxury of the time to fix them and seek resolutions.

Today's practice is going to help you do exactly that. When you don't know what to prioritise, or you're unsure of how you're going to achieve something, you're going to give gratitude to the top 3 things that you want to do in your life today.

Think of it as your cosmic wish list or cosmic to-do list for the day.

So today, we're going to answer our 3 main questions,
- What is something that made me smile yesterday?
- What can I do to make myself feel good and love myself today? And...
- What is 1 thing that I'm grateful for today?

And then once you've answered these, I want you to write down a list of the top 3 things you want to achieve today. Don't think about how they're going to be achieved if you find that you struggle for time, don't think about the HOW at all. Just make a list of those 3 tasks that in an ideal world, you'd love to complete today.

These could be things you don't have time to do or even just things you're putting off doing because they seem tedious or boring. If you struggle to think of things, go through each area of your life where you'd like something resolved or done for you on your behalf.

Maybe you want to clean your house top to bottom, but you know that'll take a good few hours, and you need to work today, and then you've got the food shopping to do, and then walk the dog, and go to the gym…

Once you've got your list of 3 things, I want you to sit comfortably and close your eyes, giving thanks and gratitude for each of these tasks having been completed, so you're basically giving thanks as though that task has been done for you or on your behalf.

I want you to imagine that every person, every circumstance, and every task on your list has been completed and the 3 things that you listed have been completed.

Your problems have been solved, and your to-do list has been ticked off. Spend at least 1 minute on each of the 3 things that you listed to really give them attention and focus. Believe each task has been completed and give great thanks and gratitude for it.

We know from studying the Law of Attraction that thoughts are magnetic, and so when we give thanks and gratitude for something having been completed on our behalf, we automatically attract everything into our lives to ensure that things are in fact completed on our behalf.

Feel free to take a picture of your daily answers if you're feeling brave enough to share, use the hashtag #31daysofgratitude and tag my main account which is @cannycrystals across all socials.

I look forward to seeing you all again tomorrow for day 19.

WHAT IS SOMETHING THAT MADE ME SMILE YESTERDAY?

....

....

....

WHAT CAN I DO TO MAKE MYSELF FEEL GOOD AND LOVE MYSELF TODAY?

....

....

....

WHAT IS ONE THING THAT I'M GRATEFUL FOR TODAY?

....

....

....

WHAT 3 THINGS WOULD YOU LIKE TO COMPLETE TODAY?

....

....

....

DAY 19

Being Grateful for Health

Welcome back to day 19 of the 31 Days of Gratitude challenge. Back on day 17, we gave thanks and showed gratitude for something that's pretty much invisible, and that was the air that we breathe. Today is looking at something else that we don't necessarily see on a day-to-day basis, but it exists, and that is good health.

Life is busy, stressful, and hectic and it can be easy to take things for granted when it feels like something is always going wrong. Even when things are going well, people tend to overlook some of the most important things in their lives. And isn't health one of the most important things in our lives?

Last year when I got struck down with Covid, I was bed bound for about a week. I lost all energy from my body and at one point when I stood up, I fell to the ground and had to crawl my way to the bathroom to be sick as I was isolated alone. I was so weak from not eating and just didn't have the energy to do anything.

When I did start mobilising around about a week later, I was breathless just walking the dog around our estate, I was breathless just walking to the toilet, and I was out of breath speaking to my Mam on the phone.

It was a nightmare, but it made me realise that we shouldn't take our health for granted.

However, it made me very aware of how our fully functioning bodies can fail. Whether it's something like

Covid, cancer, or a car accident with devasting consequences, our health can change instantly.

I promised myself that I would be much more grateful for good health and not just assume that my body will function optimally for as long as I want it to. It's so weird though because until you fully experience that ill health and you're struck down with an illness, it's only in this moment that you wish you felt better and feel thanks for all the times you felt well.

There's a great quote by Cynthia Ozick that states "When something does not insist on being noticed when we aren't grabbed by the collar or struck on the skull by a presence or an event, we take for granted the very things that most deserve our gratitude."

So today, we're going to answer our 3 main questions,
- What is something that made me smile yesterday?
- What can I do to make myself feel good and love myself today? And...
- What is 1 thing that I'm grateful for today?

And then once you've answered these, I want you to answer the following question: when did you last feel in optimal health? To some, you might answer "right now", or to some, it may have been a few years ago. Whatever your answer, think back to how you felt at that period and why you felt at optimal health.

Give thanks and gratitude to each part of your body for working cohesively to allow you to be in the best possible health that you can be. The more we give gratitude for when we feel healthy, as crazy as that sounds, the healthier we can be in our day-to-day lives.

Feel free to take a picture of your daily answers if you're feeling brave enough to share, use the hashtag #31daysofgratitude and tag my main account which is @cannycrystals across all socials.

I look forward to seeing you all again tomorrow for day 20.

WHAT IS SOMETHING THAT MADE ME SMILE YESTERDAY?

....
....
....

WHAT CAN I DO TO MAKE MYSELF FEEL GOOD AND LOVE MYSELF TODAY?

....
....
....

WHAT IS ONE THING THAT I'M GRATEFUL FOR TODAY?

....
....
....

WHEN DID YOU LAST FEEL IN OPTIMAL HEALTH?

....
....
....

DAY 20

The Gift of Time

Welcome to day 20. You're almost 2 thirds of the way through this 31-day challenge and I'm honestly so proud of you for sticking this out and making a change in your lives. Today we're going to look at the magical gift of time.

People tend to take time for granted. There are two ways that people do this. The first one is ignoring the time we have in a day and saying things like, "I don't have time."

We don't make time for important things, like exercise, self-care, learning, and spending time with those who matter to us. We all have the same 24 hours in a day, but many of us do not make the most out of that time.

Assuming that you sleep for 8 hours a day, that leaves 16 hours to live your life. 8 of those hours might be spent at work, but what about the other 8?

I know that it's easy just to sit and binge-watch a TV show, but there are so many other ways to spend our time. You could take an hour to go for a walk or get some other kind of exercise.

Cooking a nice healthy meal is a great way to spend time with your family and care for your health. That still leaves plenty of hours that we could be reading about a topic that interests us or learning a new skill.

There is time to get together with a friend and have a good time. These things could also be considered self-care, which is essential for our mental and physical health.

And then the second way we take time for granted is by thinking we have an endless supply of it. We do not.

Do you have something you want to see or do in this life? Stop putting it off and thinking that you'll do it later. There might not be a later. Instead, make a goal and work toward it the best you possibly can.

None of us are promised tomorrow, and if you have dreams, you should go for them! Live each day as if time is precious.

There's a great quote from Alex Gray that says, "It's very easy to take for granted the phenomenon that we are each alive, but we must try not to."

So today, we're going to answer our 3 main questions,
- What is something that made me smile yesterday?
- What can I do to make myself feel good and love myself today? And...
- What is 1 thing that I'm grateful for today?

And then once you've answered these, I want you to close your eyes and give thanks for all the time that you are given today and every day.

When you wake in the morning, give thanks for the remainder of the day that you're blessed with and all the things that you can achieve in the rest of that day. Be grateful for the time that you have.

Feel free to take a picture of your daily answers if you're feeling brave enough to share, use the hashtag #31daysofgratitude and tag my main account which is @cannycrystals across all socials.

I look forward to seeing you all again tomorrow for day 21.

WHAT IS SOMETHING THAT MADE ME SMILE YESTERDAY?

....

....

....

WHAT CAN I DO TO MAKE MYSELF FEEL GOOD AND LOVE MYSELF TODAY?

....

....

....

WHAT IS ONE THING THAT I'M GRATEFUL FOR TODAY?

....

....

....

DAY 21

Giving Thanks for Rest

Welcome back to day 21. Today we're going to look at giving thanks and showing gratitude for something else really simplistic in our lives that is overlooked, and that is resting and sleeping.

It's something that we all do daily, some for longer than others, but it's something that's required of our bodies to help them to function adequately and properly.

When we get decent sleep, our bodies are able to perform better and things such as our responsiveness is enhanced. When we lose out on sleep, for whatever reason it may be, we can sometimes struggle to function, and our brains are fogged. We can then fail the simplest of tasks, and a severe lack of sleep repeatedly eventually leads to a poor mood, which can lead to depression, anxiety and sadness in our lives.

So today, we're going to answer our 3 main questions,
- What is something that made me smile yesterday?
- What can I do to make myself feel good and love myself today? And...
- What is 1 thing that I'm grateful for today?

And then once you've answered these, today, or tonight, just before you wind down for sleep whenever that may be, I want you to lie on your bed and close your eyes.

Check-in with how your body feels, starting at the tip of your toes, and working up your body until you get to your head. Give thanks for the bed that you lay on, some aren't fortunate enough to even sleep on a bed.

The homeless population in the UK sleep on rough, hard surfaces; some on cold, stone floors, some on cardboard. Really give that thought some focus and feel sincere gratitude for the bed and mattress that you are lying on right now.

Then, still with your eyes closed, give gratitude and thanks that whilst you sleep, your body will rejuvenate and recharge itself, limb by limb, organ by organ, overnight whilst you lay there. Give thanks and show gratitude that your body knows how to do this without you having to give it any attention, night after night after night.

Ironically, gratitude does more than uplift someone's spirit; it produces a serenity that carries into bedtime. Scientists that have studied the effects of gratitude on sleep have found some illuminating results.

One study that included over 400 adults, 40% with sleep disorders, found that the quality of sleep was greatly improved by gratitude.

Thoughts of thankfulness for positive things just before sleep resulted in falling asleep more quickly and for a longer period. This is something you can incorporate into your bedtime routine each night. As you lay there and close your eyes, just before you drift off, give thanks for a peaceful night's sleep ahead, and in turn, your sleep quality will improve.

Feel free to take a picture of your daily answers if you're feeling brave enough to share, use the hashtag #31daysofgratitude and tag my main account which is @cannycrystals across all socials.

I look forward to seeing you all again tomorrow for day 22.

WHAT IS SOMETHING THAT MADE ME SMILE YESTERDAY?

....

....

....

WHAT CAN I DO TO MAKE MYSELF FEEL GOOD AND LOVE MYSELF TODAY?

....

....

....

WHAT IS ONE THING THAT I'M GRATEFUL FOR TODAY?

....

....

....

DAY 22

Gratitude for Water

Welcome back to day 22 of this 31-day challenge. Today we're going to be looking at something else that is widely taken for granted, and that's water.

Did you know that around 60% of our bodies are made up of water, and for us to survive and to function in fact, we need to take in water.

Water has the ability to heal! Because of the many benefits of water, it's the perfect environment for healing, recovery, therapy, and relaxation. Even the world's oldest medical literature makes numerous references to the beneficial use of the bath in treating various diseases.

Water's buoyancy creates a comforting environment to exercise and rehabilitate in. Whether you're exercising, rehabbing, or just relaxing in the water, you never have to carry the full weight of your body!

Water, whether hot or cold, when used for recovery, enhances muscle regeneration and overall recovery to increase performance.

Given these properties of water, you can both recover, relax and heal in water as well as have a challenging workout in the water, all of which is just remarkable! Water has no limitations either. Anyone, at any place in their life, can jump in a pool of water and feel rejuvenated and energized.

So today, we're going to answer our 3 main questions,

- What is something that made me smile yesterday?
- What can I do to make myself feel good and love myself today? And...
- What is 1 thing that I'm grateful for today?

And then once you've answered these, today you're going to grab yourself a glass of water. I want you to hold that water in front of you, or place it in front of you on a table, and give serious thanks for what it's capable of, thinking of all the different things I've just mentioned, as well as the fact it will keep you hydrated.

Then as you slowly start to take sips of the water, I want you to really live in the present moment and try to taste the water as much as possible, following it from passing your lips to heading down your throat and into your stomach. Think about how it's then distributed without thought to the rest of your body without you having to do a thing.

When you have a headache or hunger pangs, 90% of the time it's because your body is dehydrated – you simply need that bit of water to keep your body running efficiently. Give thanks to water and show it some gratitude today.

Feel free to take a picture of your daily answers if you're feeling brave enough to share, use the hashtag #31daysofgratitude and tag my main account which is @cannycrystals across all socials.

I look forward to seeing you all again tomorrow for day 23.

WHAT IS SOMETHING THAT MADE ME SMILE YESTERDAY?

....

....

....

WHAT CAN I DO TO MAKE MYSELF FEEL GOOD AND LOVE MYSELF TODAY?

....

....

....

WHAT IS ONE THING THAT I'M GRATEFUL FOR TODAY?

....

....

....

DAY 23

Gratitude for our Parents

Welcome back to day 23 of the 31 days of gratitude. Today we're going to be looking at our parents, and I understand and appreciate that this may be triggering for some of you, me included because I don't speak to my Dad, as he left me and my Mam when I was just 1 year old. But if you do find this triggering, please just stick it out for today and note the feelings that come up for you.

Our parents are often the two most important people in the world for us. They have given us life, and they've helped shape us into the people that we are today. They genuinely care about our health and well-being, and they have done everything under the sun for us.

If you're lucky enough to still have your parents around, that's one thing straight away to be grateful for. Many people aren't as lucky, and many others may not even know their parents. Please take today's exercise with this in mind, and if necessary, swap out what I'm going to ask you to do, with someone whom you see as the parent figure in your life right now.

There are many ways for us to show gratitude to one or both of our parents. Be open and honest with them and tell them how you feel. Simply saying "I love and appreciate you" is the ultimate way to express your appreciation for them. Letting your parents know you are grateful for the impact they've had in your life will make their day.

Regardless of whether you live with them or not, go and help them around the house. You can do the laundry, iron their clothes, or even make them lunch. This will surely help them a great deal and make a big difference.

Giving time to our parents is something that we should all do irrespective of how busy we may be. Make time for your parents and spend quality time together. Parents have so many life experiences that we can learn from. They know so much about us as they brought us up from childhood so utilise their invaluable advice.

They were patient with you every time you had tantrums when you were a toddler and when you were a stubborn teenager. Now, it's your turn to widen your understanding towards them. Being patient with them cannot be stressed enough. They deserve it!

So today, we're going to answer our 3 main questions,
- What is something that made me smile yesterday?
- What can I do to make myself feel good and love myself today? And...
- What is 1 thing that I'm grateful for today?

And then once you've answered these, I want you to also answer: what is 1 thing that makes you thankful for having your parent, parents, or parent figure in your life? This can be past or present tense.

Feel free to take a picture of your daily answers if you're feeling brave enough to share, use the hashtag #31daysofgratitude and tag my main account which is @cannycrystals across all socials.

I look forward to seeing you all again tomorrow for day 24.

WHAT IS SOMETHING THAT MADE ME SMILE YESTERDAY?

....

....

....

WHAT CAN I DO TO MAKE MYSELF FEEL GOOD AND LOVE MYSELF TODAY?

....

....

....

WHAT IS ONE THING THAT I'M GRATEFUL FOR TODAY?

....

....

....

WHAT IS 1 THING THAT MAKES YOU THANKFUL FOR HAVING YOUR PARENT FIGURE IN YOUR LIFE?

....

....

....

DAY 24

Self-Development

Welcome back to the final week of this 31-day challenge, can you believe it? You've done so well to keep this up for the last 3 and a half weeks and I'm so, so proud of you for doing so.

Today we're going to look at how we can be grateful and show gratitude for self-development.

Self-development is simply the process of learning new things and building new skills; skills that help us increase our chances of success, achieving our goals, and manifesting our dreams. And who in the right mind would say no to any of that?

The great thing is that right now in the 21st Century, self-development is available at our fingertips, most of the time for free too. Yes, we could go to the shops and buy a book, or even just buy one from a website, but there is so much free information out there too, readily available via the internet and down many other roads. I even developed cannycrystalsacademy.co.uk for this exact reason; to deliver spiritual self-development at a low cost and make it accessible to everyone.

We can easily pick up our phones or devices and listen to a self-development podcast for free. You don't need a subscription to a streaming service for that and trust me, nowadays there is a podcast episode on ANYTHING you want to listen to. I'd advise you to go and listen to "Canny Crystals: The Podcast", but honestly, there are so many to choose from, all with valuable and useful information contained within.

For those of you who would rather sit and watch something, I bet you've got a Netflix or similar subscription. There are an amazing number of things to watch on there all around self-development and spirituality which could really help you. A couple of my personal favourites are the Goop Lab with Gwyneth Paltrow, where she sends her colleagues off to indulge in different experiences like ice baths, meditation and so much more, or there are even shows like Tidying Up with Marie Kondo, where she discusses how giving thanks and getting rid of items we no longer need, allows open space for the universe to deliver more.

These are just a couple of ways that we can level up our self-development and spirituality practices. Obviously, the internet is abundant in information too, and if you're listening to this podcast, you also have access to that pretty much for free too! You might follow someone that really inspires you on Instagram and learn from them. You might choose to read a book like some of my favourites, 'Get Rich, Lucky Bitch', or the '4-Hour Work Week'.

We are so blessed to be surrounded by so much information at our fingertips that we can even access it in our beds if we really wanted to.

So today, we're going to answer our 3 main questions,
- What is something that made me smile yesterday?
- What can I do to make myself feel good and love myself today? And...
- What is 1 thing that I'm grateful for today?

And then once you've answered these, I want you to also answer: what form of self-development am I grateful for and committed to finishing? This can be a TV show, a book, a podcast, or whatever feels right to you. And I want you to really commit to watching an episode, reading a chapter, or listening to an episode today when you get time.

Feel free to take a picture of your daily answers if you're feeling brave enough to share, use the hashtag #31daysofgratitude and tag my main account which is @cannycrystals across all socials.

I look forward to seeing you all again tomorrow for day 25.

WHAT IS SOMETHING THAT MADE ME SMILE YESTERDAY?

....

....

....

WHAT CAN I DO TO MAKE MYSELF FEEL GOOD AND LOVE MYSELF TODAY?

....

....

....

WHAT IS ONE THING THAT I'M GRATEFUL FOR TODAY?

....

....

....

WHAT FORM OF SELF-DEVELOPMENT AM I GRATEFUL FOR AND COMMITTED TO FINISHING?

....

....

....

DAY 25
The Sound of Gratitude

Welcome back to day 25 and we're into the final stretch now with just a few days to go. Today we're going to be looking into the musical world and showing our gratitude for those uplifting and happy songs that take us to another place.

Our favourite melodies release dopamine, known as the feel-good hormone, which activates our brain's pleasure and reward system. Music can have a positive, immediate impact on our mental state; fast tempos can psychologically and physiologically arouse us, helping energise us for the day. Slower, meditative tunes can help us to relax and lower our stress levels.

Music is such a wonderful thing to have at our disposal on a day-to-day basis.

So today, we're going to answer our 3 main questions,
- What is something that made me smile yesterday?
- What can I do to make myself feel good and love myself today? And...
- What is 1 thing that I'm grateful for today?

And then once you've answered these, I want you to create yourself an uplifting playlist. You can either do this on a streaming service, create yourself a free YouTube playlist, or even burn a CD or cassette if you're old-school! The point of this exercise is to make you think of different songs that you can add that have the gratitude effect on your brain.

If you're on Spotify, you can search for mine for inspiration if that helps. Just type "gratitude empowerment" in the search bar and it'll bring up my playlist as well as many others.

When I'm getting ready in the morning, I like to pop my playlist on, which is full of empowering songs such as Beyonce's 'I Was Here', Sia's 'Unstoppable' and Dido's 'Thank You'.

This playlist really helps to get my vibrational state into one of gratitude that truly puts me in an amazing mood for the rest of the day.

If making a playlist isn't for you, just even pop on a CD that makes you smile and really listen to the lyrics. I guarantee if you do this at the start of the day, you'll feel gratitude for the remainder.

Feel free to take a picture of your daily answers if you're feeling brave enough to share, use the hashtag #31daysofgratitude and tag my main account which is @cannycrystals across all socials.

I look forward to seeing you all again tomorrow for day 26.

WHAT IS SOMETHING THAT MADE ME SMILE YESTERDAY?

. . . .

. . . .

. . . .

WHAT CAN I DO TO MAKE MYSELF FEEL GOOD AND LOVE MYSELF TODAY?

. . . .

. . . .

. . . .

WHAT IS ONE THING THAT I'M GRATEFUL FOR TODAY?

. . . .

. . . .

. . . .

DAY 26

Seeing Gratitude

Welcome back to day 26 of this 31-day challenge. We're onto the home stretch now and just a few more days to go until you're a true master of gratitude.

Today we're going to show gratitude for something we all take for granted – our eyesight.

I know there are a lot of people in this world who are blind. Even if you are, there are still other things you can be grateful for.

Those of you who aren't blind, however, even if you have to wear glasses or contacts, you can be grateful that you can see. Many people can't, so just think about that for a second.

Even if everything you see in the world isn't as pleasant sometimes, we can still be grateful for the pleasant things we can see, like the nice green colours of nature outside or the beautiful blue hue of the sky.

We often take our eyesight for granted as it's something that we use daily without even giving it any thought.

Did you know the lens in your eye can focus faster than any camera? Thankfully, our eyes can focus almost immediately. Otherwise, life would truly be a blur!

In fact, our eyes have some of the best auto-correct around. Whether you have glaucoma or blind spots, your eyes fill in the gaps.

In a nutshell, our eyes are incredibly adaptable. Situations and surroundings can change quickly. For example, we often go from light to dark spaces. Our eyes can adjust almost instantly. Our eyes are small but mighty.

Our eyes act like personal cameras. On average, our eyes see more than 20 million images in a lifetime. Hence, one of the reasons to be thankful for your eyes every day - your vivid memories!

So today, we're going to answer our 3 main questions,

- What is something that made me smile yesterday?
- What can I do to make myself feel good and love myself today? And...
- What is 1 thing that I'm grateful for today?

And then once you've answered these, I want you to try going about a couple of minutes of your life with your eyes closed, to truly feel what life would be like without your vision.

Obviously, be sensible about this. Don't try and walk downstairs, drive a vehicle, or do anything that could put your life in danger.

Just simply close your eyes and try making yourself a drink, or try writing yourself a note, or try typing out a note on your laptop.

Whatever you choose to do, just think of how much time and effort it takes you to do these simple tasks, and this will in turn help you to feel gratitude for the beautiful eyesight that you have.

Feel free to take a picture of your daily answers if you're feeling brave enough to share, use the hashtag

#31daysofgratitude and tag my main account which is @cannycrystals across all socials.

I look forward to seeing you all again tomorrow for day 27.

WHAT IS SOMETHING THAT MADE ME SMILE YESTERDAY?

....

....

....

WHAT CAN I DO TO MAKE MYSELF FEEL GOOD AND LOVE MYSELF TODAY?

....

....

....

WHAT IS ONE THING THAT I'M GRATEFUL FOR TODAY?

....

....

....

DAY 27

Gratitude Tastes Good

Welcome back to day 27 of this 31-day gratitude process. Today we're going to look at something else we overlook on a day-to-day basis, and that's your sense of taste.

If you've had Covid over the last few years, you'll more than likely have lost your smell or taste, I know I did, and it really affected me more than I thought it would.

For me, it was the psychological confusion of putting something that I really wanted to eat in my mouth, and then not getting that taste sensation signal to my brain. It's honestly weirder than you think.

Because I wasn't getting that hit of dopamine to the brain, it made me want to try other foods and continue eating, even though my stomach was full, because I just wasn't satisfied with the food that I was eating.

And even if you've not experienced this from Covid, I'm sure at some point in your life you've had a bad cold whereby your nose has been blocked and you've not been able to taste any of your food. I'm sure you can agree that it's not a great experience to have.

So today, we're going to answer our 3 main questions,
- What is something that made me smile yesterday?
- What can I do to make myself feel good and love myself today? And...
- What is 1 thing that I'm grateful for today?

And then once you've answered these, the next time you eat today, I want you to do it mindfully. And by that, I mean I want you to sit with your food somewhere that you won't be disturbed, so for example NOT in front of the TV.

As you put your food onto your plate, I want you to look at it, feel it, smell it, and as it enters your mouth, I want you to close your eyes and really allow yourself to taste the true flavour of your food.

When we do this undisturbed and not distracted by things like the TV, we allow our brains to fully experience the taste sensation going on in our mouths. This might sound a little weird, or even look weird that you're eating food with your eyes closed and chewing it over and over again to get the full flavour but trust me on this one.

This process truly allows us to be thankful and grateful for our sense of taste and is just one more thing to show gratitude for.

Feel free to take a picture of your daily answers if you're feeling brave enough to share, use the hashtag #31daysofgratitude and tag my main account which is @cannycrystals across all socials.

I look forward to seeing you all again tomorrow for day 28.

WHAT IS SOMETHING THAT MADE ME SMILE YESTERDAY?

....

....

....

WHAT CAN I DO TO MAKE MYSELF FEEL GOOD AND LOVE MYSELF TODAY?

....

....

....

WHAT IS ONE THING THAT I'M GRATEFUL FOR TODAY?

....

....

....

DAY 28

Gratitude for Kindness

Welcome back to day 28 of the 31-day gratitude challenge. Today we're going to look at random acts of kindness, and how we can be grateful for these in our day-to-day lives.

It may seem like there are more meaner people than kinder people in this world today, but there are still people that are exceptionally kind and really go out of their way to help you and do something nice. I like to believe that I'm one of these people.

I get a real kick out of helping others and genuinely doing kind things, that often go unnoticed, but I know inside what I've done and that gives me a great sense of accomplishment internally.

Be grateful for the kindness you receive and the acts of kindness that still happen every day. When was the last time someone did something kind to you that really made you stop and think, "Wow! That was incredibly nice of you!"

It may have been something big like someone buying you a gift without having reason to, or it could have even been something small, such as the person in front of you at the supermarket allowing you to go ahead of them and skip the queue.

Whatever it was, feel that gratitude for that experience because today we're going to repay the favour and pay it forward.

So today, we're going to answer our 3 main questions,

- What is something that made me smile yesterday?
- What can I do to make myself feel good and love myself today? And...
- What is 1 thing that I'm grateful for today?

And then once you've answered these, at some point today, I'd like you to carry out a random act of kindness.

You might decide to cook your partner their tea, or buy someone some flowers, or pay for someone's groceries, or even wash your neighbour's car... whatever you choose to do, whilst you carry out that specific activity, feel true gratitude as though it was someone else doing the task for you.

When we give out true gratitude, it is always returned to us tenfold, and so by paying it forward, we're putting out that positive energy into the universe which will be returned to us in kind.

As an additional task, maybe try doing something that goes unnoticed by the other person and see how that feels knowing that you've done something nice. Order someone a small gift but don't tell them it's from you or clean up after someone but don't mention it.

The feeling that you get inside when doing these small acts of kindness is like no other.

Feel free to take a picture of your daily answers if you're feeling brave enough to share, use the hashtag "31daysofgratitude" and tag my main account which is @cannycrystals across all socials.

I look forward to seeing you all again tomorrow for day 29.

WHAT IS SOMETHING THAT MADE ME SMILE YESTERDAY?

....

....

....

WHAT CAN I DO TO MAKE MYSELF FEEL GOOD AND LOVE MYSELF TODAY?

....

....

....

WHAT IS ONE THING THAT I'M GRATEFUL FOR TODAY?

....

....

....

DAY 29

Being Alone

Welcome back to day 29 – we're now just 3 final chapters away from the end of this challenge. Today we're going to look at something that most people hate, and that's being alone, or being on your own.

We can be constantly surrounded by people sometimes, and if you're like me, that can get really overwhelming at times. It's nice to be able to get time alone to relax or reflect, but then on the flip side of this, that can get quite lonely after a while. It's all about finding the right balance of what we prefer.

I've learned to embrace loneliness, and I've learned to enjoy and learn from it too.

Being lonely isn't a bad thing, it's an inspiring thing. I wish everyone could experience being alone for a few days because you become very grateful for what you have.

Most of us never get the gift because we're not willing to sit with our loneliness. We fill the void with Facebook, Twitter, Instagram, reality TV, and gossip about celebrities or maybe about our neighbours or co-workers. We combat loneliness with sex, food, and alcohol.

But we can't outrun loneliness or successfully hide from it because it's an integral part of us; it's hardwired into us.

If you are lonely, and you don't like it, take the time to look around at what you do have, not the people but all the things you have to be grateful for. Being lonely doesn't need to be a crutch, let it be the thing that offers a new perspective on the world.

So today, we're going to answer our 3 main questions,
- What is something that made me smile yesterday?
- What can I do to make myself feel good and love myself today? And...
- What is 1 thing that I'm grateful for today?

And then once you've answered these, at some point today, try and have some alone time. I appreciate this may be hard for you if you have small children, or pets, that rely on you. But just attempt to have some alone time.

This can be really beneficial for us as it allows our minds and thoughts to reset and show true gratitude for those people and things that we actually do have around us.

Feel free to take a picture of your daily answers if you're feeling brave enough to share, use the hashtag #31daysofgratitude and tag my main account which is @cannycrystals across all socials.

I look forward to seeing you all again tomorrow for day 30.

WHAT IS SOMETHING THAT MADE ME SMILE YESTERDAY?

....

....

....

WHAT CAN I DO TO MAKE MYSELF FEEL GOOD AND LOVE MYSELF TODAY?

....

....

....

WHAT IS ONE THING THAT I'M GRATEFUL FOR TODAY?

....

....

....

DAY 30
Inspirational Gratitude

Welcome to the penultimate day of this 31-day gratitude process. Today we're going to investigate being grateful for all the people in the world that inspire you in some way, shape or form.

Some people in this world have an amazing ability to say things that are inspiring. There are also those in this world who overcome impossible challenges that inspire us all. To you, these may be podcasters, influencers, celebrities, or public speakers – or they may even be a friend, family member, or colleague. Whoever they are, we're going to give our thanks and our gratitude to these people.

When someone has helped you, supported you, or inspired you, it's important that you tell them how much they mean to you. Now before you go spamming celebrities or public speakers' inboxes, listen on first.

If you have the opportunity to thank someone in person, it's always best to do it face to face. Thanking someone face-to-face can be a meaningful experience for both of you. It reminds you that the world isn't just made up of faceless people and that your actions have real effects on other people's lives.

If you want to show your appreciation to someone who has inspired you, a letter is the best way to do it. Not only is it a great way to express your gratitude, but it's also something the person can keep forever.

There are so many reasons why we love and admire

people, but these are the ones that come to mind when I think about why someone inspires me:

- What's special about their work?
- How do they make you feel?
- What values do they bring to the world and why do you appreciate them?
- What part of their background makes them unique or interesting to you?
- Why did they achieve what they did, and what does that mean for your life or career in the future?

People are happy to receive compliments, but they also want to know what they did that makes them worthy of praise.

When you want to thank someone, it's easy to fall into the trap of saying how much they helped you without being specific about what that help consisted of.

When you specifically tell someone what they've done for you or how grateful you are for their help, you let them know that what they're doing is important and make them feel like they're truly appreciated in life.

So today, we're going to answer our 3 main questions,
- What is something that made me smile yesterday?
- What can I do to make myself feel good and love myself today? And...
- What is 1 thing that I'm grateful for today?

And then once you've answered these, I want you to write a small thank you letter, e-mail, or DM to someone who has truly inspired you. That person may never read it due to circumstances beyond our control, but you've put that gratitude and thankful energy out into the universe by doing this task.

Feel free to take a picture of your daily answers if you're feeling brave enough to share, use the hashtag #31daysofgratitude and tag my main account which is @cannycrystals across all socials.

I look forward to seeing you all again tomorrow for the final day - day 31.

WHAT IS SOMETHING THAT MADE ME SMILE YESTERDAY?

....

....

....

WHAT CAN I DO TO MAKE MYSELF FEEL GOOD AND LOVE MYSELF TODAY?

....

....

....

WHAT IS ONE THING THAT I'M GRATEFUL FOR TODAY?

....

....

....

DAY 31

One Final Task

Welcome back to the final day of this 31-day gratitude challenge. I really hope that you've found inspiration throughout this challenge for all the different ways in life that you can be thankful for, and I hope that it's opened your eyes to things to be grateful for that you may not have given a second thought before.

From my perspective, I want to say a massive thank you to you, the listener, for sticking this challenge out and making it to the end. That's me showing my gratitude to you. I am eternally grateful.

So today, for one last time we're going to answer our 3 main questions,
- What is something that made me smile yesterday?
- What can I do to make myself feel good and love myself today? And...
- What is 1 thing that I'm grateful for today?

And then once you've answered these, I want you to find 5 minutes today where you can sit in silence, undisturbed, somewhere that is safe enough for you to do this with your eyes closed, and I want you to think back to day 1.

If I'd asked you to be grateful for 31 things on day 1 on the spot, I dare bet you would have struggled, but just sitting comfortably, I want you to give gratitude and thanks to yourself for showing up and developing yourself spiritually by doing this challenge.

Whilst you sit there, think of as many things as you can to be grateful for, including all the things in this challenge, such as air, water, music, problem-solving, challenges and anything else that comes up for you.

Write down any internal dialogue that comes up for you.

Sit in that feeling knowing that only good things can come from feeling positive, and by thinking of all the things you're grateful for, the universe can only deliver you positivity.

Once your 5 minutes have passed, know that you're a wonderful person and have so many things in your life to be grateful for, whether you believe that or not.

Feel free to take a picture of your daily answers if you're feeling brave enough to share, use the hashtag #31daysofgratitude and tag my main account which is @cannycrystals across all socials.

WHAT IS SOMETHING THAT MADE ME SMILE YESTERDAY?

....

....

....

WHAT CAN I DO TO MAKE MYSELF FEEL GOOD AND LOVE MYSELF TODAY?

....

....

....

WHAT IS ONE THING THAT I'M GRATEFUL FOR TODAY?

....

....

....

EPILOGUE

I hope that this challenge has really helped you cement the gratitude process in your brain and that you might even keep it up by thinking of something to be grateful for when you wake, up and something to be grateful for just before you sleep.

Remember, integrating gratitude into your daily life can be a powerful way to cultivate a positive mindset and increase your overall well-being.

Here are some tips to help you continue integrating gratitude into your daily routine after completing the 31-day process:

Start a gratitude journal: Continue writing down three things you are grateful for each day. This practice can help you focus on the positive things in your life and cultivate a mindset of gratitude.

Practice mindfulness: Take a few minutes each day to be mindful and present. This can be as simple as taking a few deep breaths or focusing on the present moment. Mindfulness can help you appreciate the small things in life and be more grateful for what you have.

Express gratitude to others: Take the time to thank others for their kindness and support. This can be as simple as sending a thank-you note or expressing your gratitude in person. Showing gratitude to others can strengthen your relationships and increase your feelings of happiness and contentment.

Focus on abundance: Instead of focusing on what you don't have, focus on what you do have. Take stock of the blessings in your life and be grateful for them. This can help you cultivate a mindset of abundance and positivity.

Share your gratitude journey: Share your experiences and insights with others. This can help inspire others to cultivate gratitude in their own lives and help you stay accountable to your own gratitude practice.

Remember, cultivating gratitude is a journey, not a destination. Continue to practice gratitude each day and you'll start to see positive changes in your life.

As I reach the end of this book, I'm reminded once again of the incredible power of gratitude. It's a force that can transform our lives, bringing us closer to the people we love, helping us find joy in the smallest of moments, and giving us the strength to overcome even the toughest of challenges.

In these pages, we've explored the many ways in which gratitude can enrich our lives. We've seen how it can help us cultivate a more positive mindset, deepen our relationships, and even improve our physical health. But perhaps most importantly, we've learned that gratitude is not just a feeling - it's a choice. It's something we can practice every day, in big ways and small.

So as you close this book, I invite you to take a moment to reflect on all the things in your life that you're grateful for. Maybe it's the people who love you unconditionally, the opportunities that have come your way, or the simple pleasures that bring you happiness each day. Whatever it may be, hold it close in your heart, and remember that gratitude is a gift you can give yourself, every single day.

Thank you for joining me on this journey of gratitude. I hope that the insights and practices within these pages will continue to inspire you for years to come. May your life be filled with an abundance of blessings, and may you always find joy in the simple act of giving thanks.

Don't forget to check out some of the other courses available at the Canny Crystals Academy and I hope to cross paths with you again soon!

I'm so grateful that you bought this book.

Mart